ON THE PHILOSOPHY

OF THE

University of France.

FIRST PAPER PREPARED

FOR THE

Academy of Sciences,

OF

NEW ORLEANS,

April 13th, 1874.

BY

SARAH A. DORSEY.

GEORGE ELLIS & BROTHER,
PUBLISHERS,
No. 82 Camp Street.
NEW ORLEANS, LA.,

ON THE PHILOSOPHY

OF THE

University of France,

FIRST PAPER PREPARED

FOR THE

Academy of Sciences,

OF

NEW ORLEANS,

April 13th, 1874.

BY

SARAH A., DORSEY.

GEORGE ELLIS & BROTHER,
PUBLISHERS,
No. 82 Camp Street,
NEW ORLEANS, LA.

PREFACE.

This Paper was read before the ACADEMY OF SCIENCES OF NEW ORLEANS, in order to call their attention to this eminent school of philosophy. I have used freely, not only the ideas, but the words of great Thinkers, of Mr. Janet and others, preferring them to my own *cruder* expressions. I have translated into English, the work of M. Lachelier, "Upon the Basis of Induction," which will probably soon be printed; and I am also translating the work of Mr. Fouillee upon "Free Will and Necessity, and I may add also those of Messrs. Janet and Ravaisson if I have health and leisure for this delightful labor of Love. My object is to call the attention of Thinkers to the works of these philosophers, not to gain fame for myself or credit for any originality of thought. I desire simply to serve my own people as I can best.

SARAH A. DORSEY.

Beauvoir, April 22d, 1874.

Ladies and Gentlemen.

It is with considerable alarm that I survey the audience before me! I had expected simply to read a purely metaphysical Lecture before a few scientific men, whose skill in research, and habits of logical thought, would kindly receive my imperfect suggestions, and supply all the deficiences of argument, or of interest in a subject outside, of popular reading and conversation! I shall have to solicit your forbearance in my behalf, as I am unaccustomed to appear before audiences like this· I shall therefore cast myself unreservedly upon your mercy, and beg you to pardon me if I address myself chiefly to the gentlemen by whose flattering invitation I come here to-night.

Mr. President and Gentlemen of the Academy of Sciences.

It is a great pleasure to be permitted to appear before you this evening! Recognising as I do the fact, that there is sex in all high organisms, for however true it is, that as the source of Life is one, so the source of all intellect is one; yet as life eventuates differently in different organizations, so intellect must be affected by peculiarity of the organism—at least in its manifestation and exhibition to the external world. The intellect must exhibit itself as either masculine or feminine, according to the organization through which it acts. There must be a difference, and that difference ought to be valuable and interesting to philosophers. Therefore, it is important that thinking men should know something of the thoughts of Women. I do not recognise any antagonism or any inequality in value, of the intellect of the sexes; the one is simply the complement of the other, of the Two, the intellect of Woman is probably more composed of the results of reflex action of the race, thought and habit than that of man. She seems to be in some sort, the granary of humanity! She has more of the treasures of race posited in her than man has. She has more and quicker intuition, and of what is called instinct, than he has; and philosophers teach that intuition is the ultimate product of voluntary race, thought and habit. The celebrated Dr. Meigs, of Philadelphia, in one of his Lectures to his pupils, says: "Woman is not a part of the race. She *is* the race!" He was speaking of her physically, but it seems to me the definition might be extended also to mental and spiritual, as well as to physical conditions. Woman is the depository of the germs of human thought and spirit as well as those of vital reproduction; man by his superior physical strength and will, conquers new domains of spirit and thought, wresting them from out the infinite Unknown, painfully. They, the conquered activities and impulses pass into reflex habits, and are garnered up finally as intuitions, chiefly in the daughters of his race. It is from noble mothers that noble men usually proceed. So the duties, work and education of the sexes should be, and will be different; but one is as valuable as the other; therefore I am glad to be permitted to read before you to-night, as a Woman of my people appearing before the bar of the thinking men of my own race! It is an evidence of liberal feeling upon your part, towards my sex, and so I have accepted it, not that I would desire to see Woman grow less feminine, but more so, and to see them accept frankly, not their *rights*, but *all* their RESPONSIBILITIES!

All of you must have observed, as I have done the changes in philosophy during the past twenty years. Formerly in the Schools of the United States, the Scotch metaphysics were taught. Reid and Stuart and Brown and later Hamilton. In the University of Virginia, which has a wider curriculum than any of the other colleges, they united to these, the French School of Cousin and Jouffroy. Now, nothing is read or talked of but the Insular School of Darwin, Huxley, Tyndall, Herbert Spencer, and all the rest of the English Savans, who are nearly all materialistic in their teachings, though from this, we should except partially, Herbert Spencer, who on one side, at least may be called spiritualistic, that is he acknowledges "The *probability* of a First Principle of things." Though he goes no farther than this, yet this separates him positively from Comte, and the French and English materialists, who acknowledge only the one Law of Efficient Causes, ignoring the higher and wider Law of Final Causes. If I should say in painting a picture that it was caused by the concurrence of the factors or Efficient Causes of pencils, canvass, paints, &c., it would be quite as reasonable as this, for I should then ignore in my little work, the real and final cause, my thought which willed to create the picture from the *Efficient* causes of paint, canvass, &c. There is springing up recently a strong school in England, in sympathy with the philosophy of the University of France. I am watching its progress with interest. Herbert Spencer, as I said belongs to this school in a vague way. Among the finest thinkers of this recent school, is the Hon. Roden Noel, whose last article in the Contemporary Review of Feb, 1874, on Causality in will and motion, is a very magnificent piece of philosophic reasoning.

Under these circumstances, I have thought it good to call your attention to the works of the present schoolmen of France, who are exerting to-day an influence as valuable as the schoolmen of France ever did! Since the third Christian Century all down the passing Centuries, we see what Mr. Carlyle calls so grandly "The *Torch-bearers* of Intellect" passing down from hand to hand across the Ages the fiery beacon-lights of Spiritual life and thought. You recall them! The great Doctors of Lyons, of Paris, of Avignon, of Bordeaux, of Poitiers. You remember Abelard and the Struggle for Liberty of thought in his day. They have been grand wrestlers for Truth and freedom of Debate. Those noble French Philosophers they have ever been, and they are so to-day.

I have thought it best in speaking of these Teachings to use so far as I could with some modifications, a transcription from the French of M. Paul Janet, a member of the Institute of France, who calls himself "a *Demi-Spiritualist.*"

Allow me to say here, that in the use of these words "Spiritual and Spiritualism." I do so in the pure philosophic meaning of the terms, not in their ordinary acceptation. I use them as contra-distinguished from matter and materialism. I have no knowledge whatever of the ordinary phenomena of what is commonly called Spiritualism. I accept fully the belief of Faraday and others in regard to the occult physical Laws which govern and produce these phenomena. M. Janet then calls himself a "*Demi-Spiritualist,*" not going to the extreme of the school, and therefore, perhaps is better fitted to present fairly the teachings of this school, both critically and analytically, and without partisanship, which last, though natural and valuable as a working power in practical life, is eminently unphilosophical. A true philosopher does not seek to establish dogmatically any Theory. He suggests Theories and *seeks Truth.*

This subject was discussed partially here not very long ago, when an honored member of this Academy and a life-long, dear personal Friend of my own propounded here a Theory of Two Entities. A Theory controverted by some of you It is in Essence, if not in form, an ancient and respectable Theory, coming down through venerable tradition from the East, through Zoroaster and his philosophic descendants in Asia, Europe and now in America. The most famous ancient Teacher of a similar doctrine, which has reached our time, is Lucretius in his poem De Natura, where he unfolds the secret doctrines of the Epicurean philosophy. Epicurus taught the eternity of matter in an infinite number of Entities perpetually metamorphosing, just as clearly as the materialistic philosophers of our day.

The celebrated micrographs of France, *Bichat* and Charles Robin, who have done so much for the science of general anatony, teach also a somewhat similar doctrine to that of Lucretius, (1) that of the spontaneity of the action of matter and of its Eternal metamorphoses, declaring any further knowledge of it outside of Human Cognisance.

Mr. Claude Bernard, however, equally famous in the same line of science, adheres pertinaciously to the doctrine of Final Causes, and is therefore Spiritualistic in his philosophy denying the Spontaneity of matter. (See Introduction a la medicine experimentale, in 1867.)

Mr. Martineau, in England, maintains that God had matter co-eternal with him, and yet, that Force, (or matter in motion) is will, with the element of thought left out by us, but really present. Which is contradictory, for how can Force be Divine will, if it has existed always over against Divinity? Either there are Two Divinities or there is but one.

How can there be Two Eternals, unless they are equally Infinite? How can there be two Infinites? They would be destructive one of the other—one Entity must be circumscribed and limited by the other, in order to continue to exist! However we must confine ourselves to the question of the hour. Can the Existence of Spirit be proved by positive laws without going outside of the senses? I will read you, what great Thinkers, not religious, or perhaps better to say, who are not Christian men have to say about that. Science which is unjustly charged with Irreligion is really its humble handmaiden. It is much to add to positive Science the certainty of the Existence of Spirit! C'est le premier pas qui coute!

The Philosophers of whom I am about to speak write only in foreign languages, so that their works are sealed up treasures to many who have not the two keys necessary to unlock their portals, viz: Leisure for study and some knowledge of those Languages, as well as love for Learning. I regard myself as an humble housekeeper into whose hands these precious keys have been entrusted and, most gladly I hasten to unclose the Storehouses into which I have access, at the bidding of those of my own household, for my own people, to whom I owe myself, my existence, my education, my thought, and all that I am! My object is simply to unfold the teachings of those philosophers, not to discuss or establish what they teach. That must be a separate task for each Individual to do for him or herself. We have to examine to-night a new Phase of Spiritualistic Philosophy as exhibited in the works of the present master of the University of France. We will take the three following works.

---

(1) See Richat's works "Sur Les *Tissus*."

(1) See Des Elemens Anatomigues, par Charles Robin.
"Des Tissus."
"Programme du cour d'Histologies."
"Traite du microscope."
De l'appropriation des parties organique a l'acomplisement d'actions Determinees." All by Charles Robin.

1. Report upon the Philosophy in France in the 18th Century. (Rapport sur la philosophie en France au Dixhuitieme Siecle,) by Felix Ravaisson.

2. Of the Basis of Induction (Du Fondement de l'Induction,) by I. Lachelier.

3. Free will and necessity, (La Liberte et le Determinisme,) by Alfred Foullee.

A few years since, Spiritualistic Philosophy entered upon new paths. Some youthful talents made their appearance in the daylight, some interesting attempts of speculative syntheses have been essayed, a great ardour has manifested itself in the French Normal School; all of which leads us to believe that the Philosophy of the University eclipsed for the moment by the reactionary measures of 1852, will soon recover all its strength and all its splendour. We wish to make this movement of ideas better known, which as it is shut up in the interior of the School, is not generally known and is not the less worthy of attention especially as it is probably destined to exert some influence upon the future direction of thought in France and in the world. We hope that, in spite of the dryness of the problems, our hearers will follow us willingly into these regions of lofty abstraction and forgetting for one instant the sorrowful debates of politics, that they will lift themselves up with us upon the summits of the cold, but vivifying and Eternal mountains of pure thought.

Is Spiritualism a philosophy which is able to lend itself to the changes, to the movement of Progress, and is it susceptible of taking different forms, without contradicting and without destroying itself?

A great many excellent Thinkers do not believe this to be possible.

Spiritualism they say is truth, and there is but one truth. If you admit the existence of God, the Soul, Freedom of will and a future life, you are Spiritualist; if you don't admit these, you are not. There is no medium. There is no choice possible, between yes, or no, the True and the False; one can only vary in this by deceiving oneself. Nevertheless, if instead of simply abandoning ourselves to this clear, cutting decision, we study the history of philosophy, we would readily see that in all time and in every period, spiritualism has presented itself under the freest and most varied forms. We might even postulate the contrary, and declare that it is materilism which is immobile, and which has never clothed itself with a new form, which remains always the same. All the grand ideas, all the original views of the nature of things, belong to philosophers of the Spiritualistic School, largely understood. Without going back to antiquity where from Socrates to Plotinus all the greatest schools were inspired with this spirit we find in the seventeenth Century specially, a brilliant demonstration of this free fecundity in the bosom of Universal thought. Descartes, Leibnitz and Malebranche, all three belong without doubt to the type of spiritualistic philosophy; God, the soul, the future life, are for them certain verities. We have here, however nevertheless, three systems of philosophy not only different but even opposed one to the others. The Dualism of Descartes, the dynamism of Leibnitz, the occasionalism of Malebranche, are three separate hypotheses differing in the most characteristic features, but which all expand freely in the broad field of a common faith.

How can such a liberty be refused to philosophy, when it is accorded to Theology itself: without going outside of Catholicism and beyond the 17th century, what differences were there between the Christianity of Bossuet, that of Fenelon, or that of Pascal, between the solid eclecticism of the one, the quietism of the other, the jansenism of the third! One only may be called orthodox, and that one was Bossuet (and to what degree, we may ask of him even.) But in theology you have an authority which fixes dogma; who shall decide in philosophy between the Spiritualists those which are regular, and those which are not so! We are not surprised then to find, in contemporary Spiritualistic Philosophy, that there is manifesting itself a tendency to movement, to novelties in thought, to liberty in speculation more strongly marked than in any preceeding period of time. The field of doctrine has enlarged itself and grown wide, at the risk sometimes of confounding itself with doctrines neighboring to it, but still different, this transformed and rejuvenated, but sometimes too refined, and bold thought which seems to push freedom even to audacity, has very legitimately awakened many scruples and provoked some wise reserves. But in whatever manner we may look at it, we can only rejoice to see the philosophy of the University of France enter again into the grand paths of free metaphysics, attesting its vitality by such noble and strong writings, and teaching once more with such magnificent power.

Is it of any advantage that we have a philosophy of the University, a philosophy of Schoolmen? That is precisely what we wish to examine here. The fact is that such a philosophy exists everywhere with more or less freedom, and that everywhere also, it has difficulty with an orthodoxy too jealous, which suspects her, and a revolutionary philosophy which insults her. (1) Taking the facts as they are, we will attempt to explain the different phases and degrees through which the philosophy of the University has passed, since its earliest representatives until the present actual epoch, and to show also the links which attach our new philosophers to their ancestors, and where they separate themselves from them.

It would be a grave error to believe that the doctrines of the University have always presented the characters of Unity, of fixity, of severe orthodoxy that we are accustomed to impute to it. The expression even of *Spiritualistic* School was not used in the beginning; the School at its debut called itself the Eclectic School, a more comprehensive expression than the preceeding. From the first origin of this school, we discover two different tendencies: the one more speculative, inclined towards Germany, the other more modest and altogether experimental inclined towards Scotland. From 1820, to 1830, M. Cousin has evidently inclined towards the side of Alexandrinism and Hegelianism. Jouffroy on the contrary, pushed metaphysical circumspection to a point which in another period would have made him accused of positivism. When he said for instance that the problem of the Soul was "a premature problem," when he distinguished between the questions of fact and ulterior questions, he had not very far to travel before declaring that these ulterior and premature questions were in reality insoluble questions. A very great freedom then marks the origin of contemporary spiritualism.

It was only at the end of 1830, that the new school took decided direction of the Teachings of the University. It was between 1830 to 1874 that she was constituted and took the title of the "*official* philosophy". Since then reacting partially against the too negative philosophy of Scotland, which culminated by leaning at the same time towards Hamilton, and also on the other side against the speculative Pantheism of the School of Germany, more and more exaggerated by the Hegelian left side, she circumscribed herself within the limits of a wise and correct spiritualism, putting herself in accord as much as possible with common sense and with the beliefs of natural Religion. It was at this time that she let fall into disuse the primitive name of the Eclectic School, to take the name and carry the banner of the *Spiritualistic* School of philosophy.

---

(1) See for instance in Germany, the fierce pamphlet of Schopenhauer upon the philosophy of the University (*Utter die Universitats-philosophie.*)

Nevertheless a new and important fact came now to give to this school a more severely philosophical character and to furnish her with a more solid basis, than the rather vague principles of Eclecticism could give her. This was the discovery and the publication of the writings of Maine de Biran. The fundamental idea of this great thinker is that the soul has not only conciousness of the phenomena which pass within it, but also that it has a conciousness of itself considered as force, that is to say that it feels in itself a power superior to all these phenomena, a power capable of producing them, a power which subsists singly and identically the same to itself, during all the variability of effects.

In this idea, the spiritualistic school believes it has found a principle which permits it to escape at the same time from Empiricism and Pantheism, from Empiricism because Conciousness attains to something outside of and beyond phenomena, from Pantheism since the Conciousness of an individual and personal force does not appear reconcileable with unity of substance. Such was the idea of M. Felix Ravaisson expressed in an article upon M. Hamilton in the Revue des deux Mondes, (1) and which M. Vacherot developed in a memorable article of the Dictionary of philosophic sciences. Such was the idea which made the foundation of the philosophical Teaching of the Normal School from 1840 until our day.

It is an error of M. Sainte Beuve who is ordinarily so very well informed, to have believed that the influence of Biran was altogether *recent in the University.* Nothing is less exact than to say this. The Leibnitzien and Biranian Dynamism has been I repeat it, all the philosophy of the University since 1840. The teachings of Emile Saisset, at the Normal School was essentially Biranian, and under his influence the philosophy of Leibnitz prevailed over that of Descartes. (2)

In the eyes of a badly informed public Saisset was nothing more than a most faithful Disciple of M. Cousin. In reality with a too carefully studied circumspection, which was at once the characteristic and the defect of his work, he represented a different and say personal tendency. M. Cousin in fact, while greatly admiring Maine de Biran whom he called "the grandest metaphyscian of the Century" has given but a feeble support to his ideas. He has never admitted for instance, that which was the doctrine of Emile Saisset and later of all his disciples in the University that all our metaphysical ideas cause, substance, unity, identity, duration, (excepting the idea of the absolute) owed their origin to conciousness and not to pure reason. As to the Leibnitzian dynamism, M. Cousin distrusts it exceedingly and prefers to it the dualism of Descartes, because although, always faithful to Eclecticism, he endeavours to marry the one to the other. Upon this point also the teaching of Emile Saisset was bolder than that of his master and he was much inclined to confound matter with force. In fine, he held equally as Leibnitz, doctrine of Time and Space, and that of an Eternal and Infinite Creation, a grave, and weighty Doctrine which led him later into an interesting controversy, with M. Henry Martin (of Rennes.)

If I have insisted somewhat upon the philosophic role of Emile Saisset, at the Normal School, it is because this role has been too soon forgotten; but I ought not

---

(1) See Revue 1st November 1840.

(2) In this order of ideas we should notice the remarkable work, Science, and Nature, in which the Author Mr. Magy one of the pupils of Emile Saisset has developed with a rare originality the point of view of dynamism. This work merits special examination. We have not *comprised* it in this study because it does not belong by any side, or any link to the group which we desire to observe here.

to forget in the same time, and under a freer, more lively, and more facile form, that M. Jules Simon professed analogons doctrines, but with a certain shading of Alexandrinism. Thus he taught for instance, the dogma of the Divine Incomprehensibility; a dogma which might have dragged him very far, if the time had been as favorable to hardy criticism as it has been during some years later.

We can speak only from slight knowledge of the teachings of the different masters who preceeded M. Jules Simon and Emile Saisset, in the Normal School that is to say M. M. Damiron, Ad Garnier and Vacherot; but we know them enough in their writings, to say that M. Damiron introduced into his teachings a shade of religiosity, and a very touching moral sentiment, that Mr. Ad. Garnier gave an example of the finest psychological analysis, that M. Vacherot, not yet disengaged completely from the orthodoxy of the School, then nevertheless beyond it, threw bold glances upon the ideal and speculative world, which attracted him so very powerfully.

We arrive now at the moment when the philosophy of the University was to receive at one time a double assault, and when struck both from the right and the left, it seemed to be stunned during several years, as too often happens in France to reasonable and temperate Causes.

An internal opposition was growing up, which began to undermine little by little the Edifice so skillfully constructed by the wise organizer of the official Philosophy. In the very bosom of the Normal School, until then so pacific, and so docile, new generations borne along by another *Wind* of doctrine came to astonish and disquiet the Spiritualistic Teachings. M. Taine scarcely *issued* from the benches of the College showed himself already as the Chief of a school and embarrassed the severe orthodoxy of his masters by the objections of his sharp and biting criticisms. M. About displayed his Voltairean Irony. M. Prevost Paradol, his noble but cold Spinozism. Each obeyed the impulses of his own inclination; but all, or at least the most distinguished of them declared themselves rebellious to the philosophy of Cousin, of Joufroy, of Maine de Biran, finding the one too theatrical, the other too modest, the last too abstracted, and too subtle. At the same moment the blind wisdom of great politicians, who according to Plato, "do not always know what they are doing," seconded with all their might this revolutionary movement by striking at the free thought in M. Vacherot, in Amedeus Jacques, and in giving thus to philosophical audacity, the valuable prestige of persecution; very soon after the events of 1852, one of the chairs of the Normal School was suppressed, "the aggregation of philosophy was abolished, and the teachings reduced to that of Logic only. All efforts to struggle against the current of criticism, against positivism, and pantheism, which now became the dominating philosophy of the Empire, were disarmed, and stilled in advance of it. Whoever had any freedom of spirit, was precipitated into negation and into scepticism, so many, and such efforts had been made to give to truth the aspect of constraint. All enlightened medium between faith and doubt was discredited, and discouraged, and Atheism was sown broad-cast in the interest of religion. A grand lesson forgotten now, doubtless, as so many of the lessons are, of experience and of history, and which we shall be probably called ourselves, in the interest of social order, which is said to be now so perfectly understood, to see renewed for ourselves in deplorable experience.

During this period of intellectual misery in the teaching of the Normal School, philosophy lost all its importance. The section of philosophy existed no longer, or was nothing more than an annexation generally neglected. Nevertheless this epoch was not wholly sterile since it furnished to the University M. Lachelier one of the new Masters, who is a subject for our study to-day.

In France the reactions are violent but they do not last long, there is so much of impulse in the race, and they are *incapable* of resting long in slumber or silence.

Before the reforms of M. Duruy, and those of 1857, Philosophy was suddenly re-awakened in the Normal School by the youthful brilliant, and amiable and exciting teachings of M. Caro, moderated as he was himself by the more severe, and more didactic teachings of M. Albert Lemosine. Under these two guides diversely remarkable, and of whom the qualities were so happily united, the traditions of Cousin and Joufroy were renewed, and rejuvenated; a new generation of distinguished Masters were acquired by the University and it is from it that its best Professors come to-day. In this period, this was still the spiritualism of Joufroy and of Biran which inspired the Masters and the Disciples, associated in some of them with Christian sentiments with a tender and refined morality which was represented among them by the regretted' Father Gratey.

It was in 1863, the epoch when M. Duery re-established the aggregation of philosophy (a service which the friends of free thought should *never* forget) it was then, I say, appeared the beginning of the philosophical movement which we have to study. It was in this aggregation that the new talents manifested themselves which to-day direct the teachings of the philosophy of the Normal School, and which are called to exert an immense influence upon the future of the philosophy of the University; but to understand this new movement, we shall have to go back and mount a little higher.

Amongst the philosophic writers, which had been fed by the ardent initiations of M. Cousin, there was one of the most eminent, whom public opinion placed in his school, but who held himself really aloof at some distance, and did not count himself as one of the Disciples of the Eclectic School. This was the wise and profound Author of "the Essay upon the metaphysics of Aristotle" (M. Ravaisson) this work altogether historical, did not appear to indicate a Chief of Schoolmen; some pages of a grand character, but very obscure and rapid, which formed the conclusion of the work, scarcely allowed one to perceive across them glimpses of the philosophic direction of the Author. Nevertheless the Spirit blows where it listeth. These few pages sufficed to inflame the soul and imagination of a young philosopher, M. Lachelier who was soon to be united to the master by a most intimate philosophical commerce.

Later M. Ravaisson gave a larger and richer development to his ideas in his "report upon the philosophy of the 18th Century," a very original and powerful work which excited a lively admiration in the youthful University. At last becoming President of the aggregation of philosophy as M. Cousin had been, he exerted naturally and without effort a great influence over the young intellects which of course united and impregnated themselves with all his colors. This influence also was of entirely different nature from that which M. Cousin had so long exercised.

This latter was an exciting spirit, but still domineering, he inflamed but he controlled. M. Ravaisson has an action less direct and less lively, but on the other hand, it is never to be apprehended in him, that influence may degenerate into domination. He acts if we are allowed to say it, like the God of Aristotle, who moves all, while resting tranquil himself. Such a philosophic government, if this expression can be used in regard to an action altogether intellectual, may be reconciled with perfect freedom. His pupil M. Lachelier has only gathered up his thoughts in order to transform, and to subtilise rendering them at once more precise, and more bold.

Another Thinker M. Albert Fouillee has entered upon similar paths, and encounters, in their paths, the preceeding philosophers, rather than he follows their footsteps.

All this to speak the truth, is much more confused than we represent it here. There can scarcely be said to exists a school properly so called, there is either a common tendency with great differences rather a general spirit, than definite doctrines, more of a speculative breath, more of a metaphysical liberalism, more of poetry in the expression, more of subtility and of obscurity in the thought.

Each one of these philosophers has his own thoughts, which it would be difficult perhaps to reduce to one single system, but which are nevertheless dominated by one common and fundamental maxim. This maxim is that the supreme explanation ought to looked for in that which is most elevated and not in that which is inferior; it is that the basis of things is *mind, thought, freedom* of will, and not matter, which in spite of the evidence of the blind senses is only the shadow, and appearance of reality.

II.

The philosophy of M. Ravaisson has already been the subject of a profound study due to the pen of M. Vacherot in the pages of the Revue des deux mondes. (1) He only returns to it in order to mark the point of departure of the philosophical movement, younger, and more recent, which we desire to study. This philosophy to tell the truth, is composed rather of brilliant and profound views, thrown into short and abrupt phrases, in a manner at once proud and indifferent, than of doctrines rigorously defined, severely linked, abundantly developed.

Discussion, analyisis exposition of consequences, the precise determination of ideas! in a word, all that is called in the school, the *discursive* processes, are subordinated, even sacrificed here to a synthetic and intuitive method. The Author sees all himself and affirms it is for you to see as he does; but in lack of dialectics, the brilliancy, and force of thought, the beauty of expression, the noble grandeur of philosophic emotion subjugates, us, and carries us away captive. The thought is generally obscure, and lends itself, with difficulty to analysis, one finds oneself upon the borders of *all* the philosophies, without knowing precisely with which, one has any business. If it was not for the severe language, sometimes even laboured of the Author one would be tempted to say that such a philosophy belonged rather to the regions of Poesy than to that of science. What we cannot refuse is complete possession of the imagination. Clear and exact spirits find it difficult to enter into this mode of thinking and saying, but they are precisely the very first to submit to its magic power.

Condensing as well as we are able floating and slightly nebulous thought, we believe we may say that all the philosophy of M. Ravaisson is dominated by the fundamental distinction borrowed from Aristotle of matter, and Form. Matter corresponding nearly to what is called in modern schools *substance* and form, to what is called the attributes; but whilst in modern philosophy the substance or subtratum seems to be the basis of the reality, and of true being, for Aristotle, and M. Ravaisson on the contrary, it is in the *form*, in the *essence*, that is to say in the attributes of the being that is the reality properly so called. What does it matter that the Olympian Jove was carved out of marble. It is not that fact which constitutes its beauty? Its beauty consists in the form with which it is clothed, and that form is the figure of the

(1) Revue de Juin 15, 1868.

God! Matter then is only the condition of the reality, it is not the basis of it. The more reality there is in things, the less matter there is in them, and in the Absolute reality, all matter that is to say all substance ought to vanish away. According to these truly Aristotelian views M. Ravaisson tends to suppress in philosophy all motion of substance, that is to say of dead naked *Substratum* to which comes to be added as accessories, the attributes of things.

We can readily understand the value of such views, if they are capable of being explained, defended and developed. All the force of Materialism for example, resides in the importance even perhaps exaggerated which the notion of *Substance* has taken in philosophy. Suppress that notion, and materialism has no more foundation nor reason for continued existence; but just because this negation of the idea of substance is fundamental, we wish to see it established by precise reasons, strongly demonstrated. Now the fact is that it is only in passing by, with some bold and decisive parenthesis, that our philosopher throws aside contemptuously the idea of substance; do not demand of him any discussion upon this point. Is this even one of the essential points of his philosophic doctrine, or is it one of those conjectural views which philosophers sometimes hazard without dreaming or caring what may become of them? This is what we cannot decide. The masters of philosophy are not contented to cast abroad their ideas in this negligent way. They prove them by proper reasonings, they defend them against objections, by precise arguments, they develop all the consequences to be deduced from them by a fruitful analysis. To prove, to discuss, to develop, these are the three essential conditions of a method rigorously philosophical. I acknowledge that before making use of these processes, one must be capable of thinking, and that the philosophy of M. Ravaisson is nourished with powerful thoughts but nevertheless these are after all, simply materials, very precious materials that he does not choose to cut, and polish himself, and which he abandons with admirable indifference to their uncertain destiny.

I will say the same of another idea which M. Ravaisson borrows from Aristotle, and which he drops carelessly in passing onward. With Aristotle he distinguishes the efficient cause from the final cause, like him also he accords to this latter a very high importance in philosophy. He goes so far even as to affirm that at bottom efficient Causes reduce themselves to, and are contained in final Causes, and that the latter are the only true Causes. You can readily see the gravity of this doctrine. Whilst the other contemporary schools, resting, or pretending to rest upon the positive sciences, tend to destroy the idea of final Causes out of science, and out of metaphysics, as a superannuated prejudice, it is certainly good strategy to take the offensive, and mining deeper than ever into the very thoughts of the adversaries, than they have done for themselves, to prove to them that what they call the efficient cause, is in reality only the final cause itself, as also what they call matter is in reality only force and intelligence.

Nothing is more important than that here instead of an assertion, we should have a demonstration, and it is always just here that the omission occurs. These are views rather than Theorems. Any one may think of things in this manner if they like to; but one is not *obliged* to think them so. Still we declare again for the second time, that Dialectics are not all of philosophy, and even that the Thinker is the Superior of the Dialectician, but a great master should be both. Philosophy is composed of thoughts and of arguments. Arguments without thoughts as in scholasticism are "empty" but thoughts without arguments are "blind" if we may borrow from Kant the celebrated Distinction which he applies to the necessary union of Conceptions and of Sensations.

Although we see that the basis of the ideas of M. Ravaisson are borrowed from *peripatetsm* we may say that it is a *peripatetism* modified, and transformed by the influence of Descartes, of Biran and of Schelling. It is the philosophy of Aristotle Spiritualised in some degree by its contact with modern philosophy. The general character of this philosophy, since Descartes, is to place itself at the subjective point of view, in the very centre of Conciousness, in the perception of the self or the Me M. Ravaisson admits this fundamental thought with instance. It is in the concious-ness of the intelligence itself, that it has of itself, that he finds the type of all reality. He insists positively upon this thought of Biran, that the soul sees in itself not only its phenomena, but its existence, its causality, and if one must admit the notion of substance, its substantiality. He goes even farther than Maine de Biran, and and whilst the latter limits the domains of conciousness to our personal activity, and puts us only in communication with the Divine and the Absolute through a sort of mystical illumination, M. Ravaisson ventures this bold, perhaps audacious, but still very profound thought that the soul in taking Conciousness of herself, takes also cognisance of the Absolute. It is God himself we feel within us, according to the doc-trine of theApostle "in Deo vivimus," and nature like us is full of God.

As M. Vacherot has already sagely remarked, the spiritualism of M. Ravaisson and of his disciples, takes the problem just as the Materialists pose it; but in an adverse sense, whilst the latter explain all by the ultimate *matter*, the former explain all by the ultimate *form.*

For the one school the superior forms are only combinations of inferiors; for the other the inferiors are only degrees of the superiors. Nature in either bypothesis is only a scale of graduated forms, passing on from one to the other in a continual progress; but this progress is for the one only a complication of happy accidents, for the other a perpetual ascension towards the better. The physical forces as well as the chemical, life, instinct, activity, love, even liberty of will, are only successive appari-tions of that Universal Spontaneity of which the source is in God. The material is already Spiritual, the spiritual is already divine, God and the Soul are the objects of interior experience; THEY ARE FACTS.

It is for this that M. Ravaisson calls his doctrine a positive spiritualism and he opposes this doctrine to what he calls the demi-spiritualism of the Eclectic School declaring in a very sarcastic, and somewhat haughty manner, his separation from this School, and appearing to have it specially at heart, not to be confounded with it.

Certain timorous spirits might reproach the preceeding views with coasting very near to Pantheism, so near that sometimes one believes it really to be the same; but we advise, that we should not abuse ourselves with this spectre of Pantheism, which ends by paralysing all philosophy. For fear of seeing pitfalls everywhere around us, we are afraid either to speak, or think, or budge.

If one expreses a few doubts as Socrates did, you are declared to be a sceptic.

If you accord something to the science of matter, you are a materialist. If you essay to conciliate determinism and liberty, you are a fatalist. If you see God in every-thing, you are a Pantheist.

In truth this perpetual invocation of bad doctrines has something irritating in it, and ends generally by giving one a taste for them, as in Politics one becomes revolutionary simply from hearing the Revolution perpetually denounced by an absurd fanaticism.

We are permitted here to state the solid and profound distinction of a German philosopher named Krause between Pantheism, and this that he calls *Panentheism.* It is one thing to say, that everything is God, and *another* to say that all is in God. M. Ravaisson is then a Panentheist; but nothing authorizes us to say that he is a Pantheist, and for ourselves, we follow him willingly over this slippery ground. * *

If there is to-day a Thinker in the University of France to whom belongs legitimately the Leadership of spiritualistic thought, that thinker is the Author of the "Report upon the philosophy of the 19th Century", M. Felix Ravaisson.

III.

M. Lachelier is a disciple of M. Ravaisson; but he is an emancipated disciple, bolder than his master, and of a different stamp. His method, his turn of intellect, even his doctrine is different. There is nothing in common between them but a certain general direction of thought, the *use* of certain formularies, and an analogous final tendency. The Author proceeds from the first in an entirely different manner. Instead of those jets of lights (electric) interrupted by obscurity, which characterise the intuitive and bold method of M. Ravaisson, here on the contrary we find a systematic and persistent thought, which follows without any break, from the first to the last line of that remarkable work "*Upon the Basis* of *Induction*!" This Chain is so close, that it forms in some sort, one single knot, or rather a series of knots tied one upon the other, which it is necessary to untie with one single effort from the beginning to the end of it. Not an instant of repose for the intellect, nothing for solace, nothing for light is granted. Those who have heretofore accused the philosophy of the University of being a literary, and superficial philosophy, have no longer room for complaint, here philosophic severity is pushed to sterness almost forbidding.

Although remarkably written, in a strong fine style, sometimes even highly colored, the work of M. Lachelier is about as easy to read as an Algebraic treatise, with this difference that the Algebraic language, being of an absolute precision, only requires, to be understood, attention and patience, whilst the indeterminate signs of the language of philosophy obscure and fatigue the thought, unless the Author comes to you and perpetually, with his explanations, in order to fix their meaning, which M. Lachelier never condescends to do, and for this reason his book so interesting in its subject, imposes an excessive fatigue upon the mind, which the Author could have prevented by a little complaisance.

This laborious method has its source in an intelligence, naturally searching and profound, which ploughs so deep that one is disquieted and asks whether he really has solid earth beneath his feet, one is borne along from bed to bed of underlying strata of thought without knowing whether there is any solid last one beneath. When we believe we have gotten possession of truth, we find it is only a phantom and that beneath this shadow there is another truth still more true, which is yet nevertheless as much a phantom, as the first so that even when the philosopher stops and says or seems to say to us: "Here it is, we have reached it"—We mistrust him and say involuntarily, that it only depends upon the will of the Enchanter, to make this last form of Truth vanish like all the preceeding ones, and to abandon it as to a night, without any bottom to its darkness. Thus although the Author in this work searches above all, to discover a solid and immoveable basis, the impression we receive is one of a transcendent scepticism with mysticism in perspective as its ultimate goal. And yet the charm is so powerful of an active and living thought, that one likes better the risk of "this infinite course" across things, as Plato says, than the ordinary routine of dogmatism.

As to M. Lachelier's doctrine, it seems to travel far from that of his early masters. He has long since passed out of the peripatetic dynamism, with its tinge of Alexandrinism, which seemed to be the teachings of M. Ravaisson. This dynamism even when enlarged is still one of the appearances or phantoms, which veil truth beyond themselves, in the Kantian idealism.

If we are able to condense the philosophy of M. Ravaisson in the words "Spirit is everything" we can condense that of M. Lachelier in these. "Thought is every thing", at least for all that is possibly the object of human science, for perhaps, there is something beyond which, there is neither thought nor the object of thought. This domain left untouched, the hypothesis adopted by M. Lachelier is that which explains the possibility of human Science, not by the objective laws of nature in so much as they are capable of being known to us, but by the subjective laws of our thought, in so much as it is capable of knowing. We know that the supreme originality of Kant, was in bringing what was without, to the within, of the conditions of existence, and instead of subordinating thought to objects to have subordinated objects to thought. In a word according to Idealism, I do not think nature because she exists, she exists because I think her. (Swendenborg adopted this philosophy.)

The Laws of nature in their supreme expression, and their essential verity, are only the Laws of our own personal thought. Now these Laws branch out according to M. Lachelier into two fundamental ones; the Law of Efficient Causes, and the Law of Final Causes. The first governs the inflexible determinism of Nature. It is in virtue of this Law that all phenomena is comprised in a series where the existence of each term or factor, determines that of the term or product which follows it.

According to the second Law, of final Causes, all phenomena is comprised in a System where the idea of all, determines in advance, the existence of the parts. These two Laws, according to Leibnitz and Kant, are reciprocal, one to the other: they are two series in an inverse sense, the one descending the other ascending, that which is cause in the one, is effect in the other and vice-versa.

What is the basis of the Law of efficient Causes? It is that, without this Law thought would be impossible. The fundamental condition of thought is unity. I cannot think without linking one idea upon another idea. Upon what then does this *Unity* of thought rest? Upon the Unity of the Universe doubtless, "for the question of, to know how our sensations unite to form a single thought is the same as that of to know how all phenomena can form one Universe. (1)"

"Now the unity of the Universe is itself only possible on condition of forming a necessary chain, as every phenomena given, links itself always, rigorously to a preceeding phenomenon. Without such a chain there is no unity in the Universe, no unity in thought, in consequence, no thought at all. Such a chain is nothing more than the laws of causality. In fine, whence comes this inflexible chain of phenomena,

(1) It seems that the Author here enters into a flagrant vicious circle, for after having said that we must explain the object by the subject, it is here the contrary, for in nature that is to say in the object, he seeks the explanation of the thought. But this vicious circle is only apparent, for it is evident that there is question here of only an ideal universe, only as it is thought of. One sees in this example the cause of obscurities in our Author. He makes no effort to foresee the confusion which he might produce in the mind of his readers. It is your business to follow him if you are able to do it.

and why are we not able to think of one of them, except upon condition of having previously thought the other preceeding it. Is it not, that these two existences are only properly speaking, but two distinct moments of a single existence, which continues by transforming itself from the first into the second. "All phenomena, are they not one single and the same phenomenon at once one, and diverse, and of which the continuity conciliates itself perpetually with change? This phenomenon is motion." All phenomena then are movements of force or rather a single movement which goes on as much as possible in the same direction, and with equal rapidity whatever may be the restraining laws according to which it transforms itself.

The Author admits in all its extent, the Cartesian mechanism, and he follows this principle throughout all the degrees, not only in the inorganic world, but also in organised and living nature. He recognises that such a conception, if it should be exclusive, would be a sort of "Idealistic materialism," (but we must not forget that it corresponds only with *one* of the laws of our intelligence that of efficient Causes. We have yet to explain the law of final Causes.)

What is the reason of this second law?

The Author serves himself still with the preceeding principle, that is *"the necessity of Unity in the thought*: but here it is (of Unity) of *a different species* that he speaks. The first is only in reality a superficial and external Unity. What in truth is motion? It is nothing more than the possibility of passing without interruption from one place to another in Space and Time. It is an empty unity and without intrinsic value. A thought which reposes only upon mechanical Unity glides over the surface of things without penetrating into the things themselves. Stranger to reality, she lacks reality herself, and remains only the empty husk of a thought. We must then find a means of rendering at once, reality to thought and intelligibility to that reality, in substituting to Unity purely external of universal mechanism, the internal, and organic unity of a systematic harmony. "Without this principle, thought may exist, but this purely abstract existence would be for it a state of exhaustion and of death." The law of final Causes gives life to thought in giving it also to nature.

Once in possession of this principle, our Idealist philosopher pretends to re-discover one after the other all the truths of which he had made abstractions in the first phase of his researches. Thus he seizes, or *thinks*, he seizes hold of the objectivity of nature, the principle of force, of activity, of spontaneity, of liberty, which elevates the human soul of which he always maintains the spirituality from his point of view. In a word as he expresses it himself, if the principle of Efficient Causes conducts to a sort of "idealistic *materialism*," the principle of final Causes leads us up to a "spiritualistic realism." Still even this is not the last word of the philosophy; this is only a second stage which of itself necessitates a third.

"This second philosophy", says the Author in concluding, "in subordinating mechanism to finality, prepares us to subordinate finality itself to a superior principle, as if to leap across the limits of thought by an act of moral faith, as well as across the limits of Nature." It is upon the threshold of this third world, announced in such a mysterious manner that the Author pauses. He only wishes to explain scientific possibilities; but he lets us see that above science, there is something else, that is to say there is *morality* and *religion*. Shall it be then, according to him, that philosophy cannot reach any further, and that all its duty is to prepare the thought, for its own annihilation, in such a manner, that she is only, all at first; to become nothing afterward? We are not able to say, the Author having refused us any further explanation of this new world of which he opens a glimpse for us without wishing to enter it himself. Without entering it any farther than he does, and confining ourselves within the limits he has fixed, let us essay to tell how far we believe we can follow him in these seducing Speculations, and where the limits are, where severe reasoning compels us to stop in spite of him.

Doubtless it is impossible to-day to a reflecting mind, not to take count of the powerful revolution made by Kant in philosophy. Either philosophy is only an illusion, a vain science or all the grand phases of its development correspond to journeyings towards truth, to degrees of Truth. Every grand philosophic system is a particle of Truth Eternal. In this maxim was laid the solid basis of Eclecticism, and we energetically hold on to it. The idealism of Kant had then its truth; but it was neither probable, nor necessary that it should be all the truth. Things, at least external things, are only known to us by the effects they produce in us, that is to say by our affections, by our sensations which by a common accord, are eminently inevitably subjective, because a sensation can only be the mode of a subject which feels. We know otherwise that the sensations are only affections produced upon each species of sense by a common cause, viz: motion.

Let us admit, if it is desired, that motion is nothing more itself, than an ideal and subjective phenomenon, let us admit that Space and Time despite their absolute character are only forms of sensibility; let us go still further, the understanding itself, being always mixed with sensibility, impregnated with sensibility to a depth which no one can determine, let us suppose that primordial laws of the understanding are themselves modified by that influence. Let us push idealism as far as any one wants it to go; there will always remain something outside of it, which cannot be reduced into the Ego which thinks. This is really, and solely. The *reality* of the sensation, it is its very existence, because no law of our mind, no condition of human thought can compel a sensation to surge up within us, simply because our understanding has need of it. It is also in the second place the order of our sensations, I mean the necessary relations which exist among them, and of which the relations of time are perhaps only symbolic expressions, but which ought to have an intrinsic and objective reason, for how, I demand, and why does our sensibility obey our understanding? Why is the order of our sensations, the faithful reproduction of a logical plan, predetermined by the Intellect? We should not forget, that our sensations are passive, are involuntary; they have their origin in Causes that escape us, and of which the direction is beyond our power. What then is the mysterious power which creates in us sensations, after its own law, at the moment and in the measure that our intelligence demands them? To give a precise form to this fundamental difficulty, the rational laws of our intellect, exact, that such a Star should be in the heavens at such a place at such a moment of time; well! by what mystery does sensibility, fatal and blind faculty as it is, outside of our own power, make to rise up within us the *sensation of a Star* precisely as fixed a Priori by the understanding? Our sensations in truth could very well form only *a chaos*, andthe need of our intellects for order and unity would not suffice to subdue to this order an undisciplined matter, if she herself, in the depths of her essence did not contain something which responds to this law of unity. In a word we accord that the world in which we live may truly be a phenomenal world of which the essential basis is unknown to us; but we feel at the same time that this world attaches itself to this *Essential basis* in a rigorous manner, just as the phenomenal or apparent heaven which falls under our senses is rigorously the astronomical Heavens which science conceives and demonstrates, and which nevertheless is different from it: thus subjectivism and objectivism are conciliated for us. The deeper we go into these matters the closer we approach to the essential reality without ever attaining to it.

But it will be asked, why this unknown cause of our sensations which we call the object, is not the Ego itself, the mind itself, the subject which thinks? Why is not Imagination the productive faculty of the Universe? We pass here from the Hypothesis of Kant to that of Fichte, and although M. Lachelier does not explain himself clearly upon this point, we have reason to think that he attaches himself rather to the second than to the first hypothesis. But we see here only a question of words and not a new light upon things. *If the Ego posits the Universe, or creates it, it is evidently without knowing it, because none of us has ever had the consciousness of being the creator of the Universe. Now an Ego of which I have no consciousness, I call a non-Ego. Everything which passes out of consciousness, passes out of the domain, of the subject, and vigorously speaking, should be called an object. That which philosophy calls Existence in opposition to thought, is precisely that unconscious something, if not unknown to itself, at least for us unknown, which is the cause of the order and the Existence of the Universe. Whatever may be the essential and objective identity that may exist between the subject and the object, between the infinite and the finite, the *opposition* remains unless we confuse all ideas by an arbitrary language.

We must carefully distinguish also, otherwise, the degrees in Idealism, and should understand clearly what is meant by intelligence, by thought! Are we speaking of human or absolute thought, of thought in itself? For Kant it is the first, viz: human thought. For Fichte, the Ego was at first only the Human Ego; later in his second philosophy it became the divine Ego, the absolute Ego. For Schelling and for Hegel it is the absolute thought, the absolute idea which was the only reality. In such a system it is evident that human spirit, inasmuch as it is circumscribed and limited by consciousness has a perfect right to oppose it itself. The Universe as a non-Ego–as an object, the idea or the absolute, being precisely this, is the objective basis which we conceive immediately for our sensations. According to this hypothesis, not only is the object affirmed as really existing, but may perhaps be known in itself, and in its essence by an absolute method. The objective reality of the Universe is not only not put in question, but it seems to be even better guaranteed than in any other system, since the rational Laws to which science refers, as all cosmical phenomena, are not only pure connections between the Causes and unknown Substances, but these Causes and these Substances themselves. It remains to inquire now, why one should call by the name of thought, objective laws which have no consciousness of themselves, and if the essential character of thought is not consciousness. If we are told that in thought, we must distinguish the basis and the form, the thought and the thinking, (cogitatum et cogitans) it is a distinction which is precisely the same thing as the classical distinction of the intelligible, and the Intelligence. To say that thought is everything or everything is thought, then, is to say that everthing is intelligible, and the intelligible is the basis of everything. Is it worth while to employ such arbitrary formularies, such strange ones in order to say simply what has never been an object of doubt to any metaphysician?

We cannot accord then to the subtle Author of the Basis of Induction (Fondement de l'Induction) that "all is Thought," at least without taking the word in a sense so large and so vague, that it will signify exactly the opposite of all that we are in the habit of *ascribing* to it. At least we must distinguish the objective thought

---

*Swedenborgianism.

from the subjective thought, and call this objective thought however it exhibits itself under the form of Extension, *matter*, and subjective thought when it exhibits itself by consciousness to itself, we call *Spirit*—and we also distinguish the one from the other in the fact, that the first appears to us always in a condition of dispersion and plurality, and that it finds unity only outside of itself in the Spirit, which thinks of it, whilst the Spirit characterized by self consciousness appears to us in a permanent state of concentration and finds unity in itself. To be Spirit, is to be One; to be matter is to be several. Thus the distinction between matter and spirit should still continue no matter how far we push the system of identity. It is the same with the individual, and the whole individual personality cannot comprehend itself without a principle of distinction which limits it, and circumscribes it within the Universal Unity. The plurality of substances cannot explain the Unity of the Ego. The Unity of substance cannot explain the plurality of the *Egos*.* Thus the primitive Unity called God, Substance, Force, Thought, Idea, Will, what you please, has let come from itself, secondary entities called souls, which distinguish themselves from the supreme cause in one way by the consciousness of their individuality, and in another from the coexistent Pluralites called bodies, by a consciousness of unity. * * * * *

IV.

M. Alfred Fouillee, colleague of M. Lachelier at the Superior Normal School, and who divides with him the present direction of our Philosophical teaching, is a young writer who has put himself in the very first rank by two works diversely though equally remarkable. The one historic, the other theoretic, one upon the Philosophy of Plato, the second upon Freewill and Determinism. The talent of M. Fouillee is of another species than that of M. Lachelier, and his philosophic doctrine does not present the same characteristic. The one as we have seen is rigorously what is called an Idealist. The other a Spiritualist properly understood, M. de Lachelier has more strength, M. Fouillee more breadth. * * * * * * * * * *

We have condensed the philosophy of M. Lachelier by the formula "all is thought" we may do the same with M. Fouillee by which "all is freewill," at least this seems to be the tendency of his last work for in the first upon the philosophy of Plato he seems to have taken intelligence as the principle instead of volition. The supreme principle, according to this, is the principle of sufficient reason.

"There is reason for everything" he says with Leibuitz, "there is idea for everything" he says with Plato.

In fine the principle of causality is for him only a particular case of the principle of reason. But in his recent work, it seems that volition takes the place of intelligence.

The Law of Causality which was formerly only a consequence is become a principle, idea is subordinated to Liberty.

This seems to be the doctrine of several of our philosophers, among others of M. Lecretan of Lausanne, which begins to exert much influence over our youthful

---

*I beg pardon for this word I could find no other?

philosophers. In his Philosophy of Liberty, M. Lecretan teaches that the essence of Deity is absolute Liberty, and that all his attributes are only different names for that Liberty. Although very bold, the philosophy of M. Lecretan is attached to Christian tradition, and it has a profoundly religious character. Another philosophy entirely different rests also upon this principle, that is the pessimist philosophy so misanthropic of Schopenhauer. He also subordinates intelligence to will, which is the only reality in itself, intelligence being only its mode of apparition. To this doctrine of the will Schelling also is attached by his second philosophy, which is according to him the positive portion of his system, the first forming only a negative, and abstract portion, M. Ravaisson in his Report seems also to incline towards this principle. M. Fouillee makes intelligence come from will, considering the last as an absolute act, not determined, but determining: which consequently commands motives, instead of being guided by them. If we consider for instance not human but Divine Liberty, we must recognise that the philosophy of the School gives a feeble part to this Liberty in the act of creation. It is repeated continually that God created the world not out of nothing, as if that was a great miracle? What does it matter what the world is made of? It is the *idea* of the world that is the wonder; it is not the stuff of which it is composed. He who made the marble, is he greater than he who made the Statue? This is always the error of the materialists who believe matter to be more important than form;-we inscribe then as false this maxim of the schools. That God created existences and not Essences, admit with Plato that the essence of Created things existed eternally, and that God only produced externally this pro-conceived world, this anticipated photography;-associate with him even under the title of Ideal, such a world or even worlds to infinity, which he inhabits without having willed them, this is as Spinoza objected to Leibnitz, and Fenelon to Malbranche, this is, only to reduce God to submission to a Fatum. It is a sort of Pantheism which subordinates God to the world since the image of the world is necessary to his existence. It is only necessary to give us knowledge of this existence as human. Doubtless truth cannot be the object of a free act of God, nor, of any power in the world. Doubtless a triangle being given, it is necessary of all necessities that its three angles should be equal to two right angles. But is it necessary that a triangle should be given? That's the question. A triangle is the synthesis of three lines distributed in a certain manner; now is this synthesis necessary, *eternal* and absolute, existing of itself? Does it not necessitate a foregoing activity, a productive power, in order to approach these three lines in such a mode, that they cut one another! We distinguish among human genius, those who copy, and those who create. Cannot the Divine activity create without copying? To create is to invent; invention is an act of will and of power, and not intelligence solely. The Divine model himself-The Paradigm of Plato, that which he calls, the Autozoon the animal in itself, is then himself the work of the divine will. He is, if you choose to say it, engendered, begotten but not created. It is the first born of God. Prototoxos protogenes, and it is perhaps this that is signified by the profound mystery of Christian Theology, namely *that the Father begot the Son.* There are two problems in philosophy, to distinguish, and to unite or combine. Ancient Spiritualism distinguishes too much, and neglected the links between things. Modern Spiritualism confounds all too much perhaps, and lets escape differences and oppositions.

M. Janet whose analysis of these three great philosophies we have concientiously followed is regarded himself, M. Saint Rene Taillandier, declares, as "one of the most sincere Thinkers, one of the most subtle, and penetrating Dialecticians of the present day." He says. "M. Paul Janet is one of those Thinkers, whose wealth and splendour become multiplied in proportion as their liberty increases." That he is "a true model of a philosophic Tactician." That "M. Paul Janet is no Partisan. He searches into the laws which govern our actions, he lifts himself up to the law which includes all others, he examines that law, he sounds its profoundest depths, and engaged in this study, he is resolute to follow *wherever* it may lead him."

M. Janet's recent great work upon "The Moral, and Free Thought" has made a profound impression upon the world of philosophers. He is not a Christian, although his conclusions after the most vigorous logic, land us somewhere very near to Christianity. He indeed speaks rather scornfully of the present phase of Christian Theology, but he reaches the ultimate facts which are the foundation of our religion and which seem to necessitate the Christian faith. They are the fundamental truths of the Christ-Spirit, and Teachings of the Divine master.

In this most remarkable book, which goes a step farther than Ravaisson, Lachelier or Fouillee, have gone *as yet*, M. Janet begins by declaring his repudiation of the meaning given to the noble words "Free Thinker, and Free Thought" by ordinary and vulgar acceptation. According to the ordinary use, the Free Thinker is the one who believes in nothing, and the fewer the beliefs the more claim one has to this Title. The sum of belief being greater in the Catholic than in the Lutheran, less great in the Deist than in the Lutheran, less great in the Atheist than in the Deist, it follows that the Atheist is supposed to think more freely than the Deist, the Deist than the Protestant, and the Protestant than the Romanist, and on this scale there is still another degree. The absolute sceptic would be considered the freest of all Thinkers. He believes in nothing, and even above the absolute sceptic modern philosophy reveals spirit still more disenthralled from all principle, and all law, for example, the Pessemist like Schopenhauer who discovers that Creation is the work of a will without intelligence. The Pessemist who despises and scorns the Universe, who scorns himself, who scorns even the scorn of which he is himself the object, and who aspires only to re-enter into nothingness. When one has arrived at this point: Spernere mundum, Spernere se ipsum, Spernere Sperni, taking it in Schopenhauer's sense, he has reached the last term of philosophic, and moral negations. *Is this free Thinking?* M. Janet draws with his usual precision the necessary consequences of this style of definition, and resumes the discussion by saying:

"There are incredulous men, who far from thinking freely, *do not think at all*, but accept objections as servilely as other men do dogmas; There are believers on the other hand who have a custom of the boldest, freest thinking: *It is not the thing thought which constitutes freedom, it is the manner in which the thing is thought out:*"

"Free thought, so far as it concerns humanity," says Saint Rene Taillandier, is that which is the most liberated from the servitudes attached to human conditions. These numerous servitudes may be reduced to two Categories, servitudes of ignorance, and servitudes of passions, those which oppress intelligence, those which mislead sensibility. Imagine a soul strong enough to silence all its passions, except the love of Truth,-sufficiently endowed, to augment without ceasing its treasure of knowledge, that is to say, to diminish ceaselessly its fetters, would not that be a free thought? and would it be a soul necessarily of smallest faith and fewest beliefs? Quite the reverse! It would be a soul which possessed more richly than any other, positive and exact affirmations where narrower spirits less disenthralled from their chains, feel obliged to deny and to doubt. This grander and wiser soul will seize the marvelous relations in the great Universal harmony. He will be a *believer*, in so far as He is a *Seer* (*ce sera un croyant parceque ce sera un voyant.*)

"The Free Thinker then is He who has liberated himself from the fetters of doubt, from the chains of negation and possesses most number of his beliefs through his reason as well as through his heart."

After the ordinary definition the Thinker is freer as he becomes poorer, but after that of M. Janet and Mr. Taillandier, he is only a true free Thinker, who sees his riches multiply in proportion to the growth of his liberty. No one applies the rule of Descartes more rigidly than M. Janet in this great work. Upon "*The moral,*" M. Janet abandons without hesitation the ordinary substratum laid down by Kant and Fichte, and other writers, of an *independent morality.*

What idea have they he declares, of the cosmos and of the harmony of things? Has science discovered anything whatever in the universe, wholly independent and isolated? Nothing is isolated, nothing is independent, and in the moral as in the physical world, every effort of the genius of man discovers relations unsuspected until the instant, which force us to suspect others, and aid us to conceive a distant idea of a prodigious chain of moral forces. Emanual Kant and Fichte derive the idea of moral law from the idea we have of our liberty. The liberty of man They say, "supposes a law necessarily: he must obey that law, duty exacts it, orders it, and it is this obedience which is precisely man's happiness." In other terms good does not exist in itself, it is the result of the accomplishment of duty, in another word it is not good which is the principle of duty, it is duty which is the principle of good. This sombre and austere moral, a philosophic jansenism which holds man under the yoke without making him comprehend or love the Law, is rejected by M. Janet. "Kant is right, he says when he establishes so powerfully the obligatory character of the moral Law: but he is wrong, a thousand times wrong when he makes of this Law a sort of abstract Tyrant, an imperative idea, which we find in ourselves, but which does not represent to us anything living, nothing substantial, no reality superior to ourselves. It is because the rigorous Thinker of Konigsberg was always possessed by the thought that we were not able to go outside of ourselves. A profounder psychology, proves on the contrary that we cannot, regard ourselves without going above and beyond ourselves.

"The internal master," says Fenelon, "is at the same time the Universal master." The voice which speaks to our consciousness is the voice which governs the world. We must break loose the fetters of Kant then, and substitute to the idea of an abstract law, the idea of a *living* law, put in the place of "*Sic volo sic jubeo*" the sublime and beneficent end which we are commanded to grow towards.

But what is this reality, this living reality which we *ought to* pursue? What is this superior end, which we ought to try to attain to?

What are, in one word, the benefits, in which are born for us both duty and virtue? M. Janet comprises all in one word. "*Perfection.*"

It is towards the perfection of our faculties, of our nature in its greatest excellence that we are obliged to tend in all of our efforts! and in what consists this Perfection?

Where is the sign of this excellence? In a certain sense this has been declared by all philosophers from Aristotle to Leibnitz. But M. Janet makes it his own in fully expressing the joy which this view of the moral law causes to enter the heart of man. One should no longer speak of joy or of pleasure in the sense of the Utilitarian or of abstract legislation as imposed by Kant. We have here a living Law, an august ideal which attracts and charms us. The fine joy of growth towards good, beauty and harmony! The joy of God!

Some teachers lower the destiny of man, others over cloud it and make it gloomy; but for those to whom it unfolds itself, from progress to progress, from perfection to perfection, who believe they can acquire a personality even higher, richer, more radiant, and thus become participants in the immortal good, happiness and virtue are one, and the same thing.

But says M. Janet, this must not be a morality of pride and exclusiveness. Egotism under any form remains egotism. "The true human perfection," says M. Janet, the ideal excellence of human nature, consists in forgetfulness of self in others." As a type of this moral sublimity he instances maternal love, and the first characteristic of this ideal grandeur, is at once to attain to, and to ignore the very perfection that it realises:—a mother who suffers the agonies of death for her child, the *Mater dolorosa* does not know that her sorrows are sublime, and are her maternal glories. She suffers divinely, and this suffering for another in another which forgets itself wholly, is the seal of a nature which belongs not only to the world of sense, but to the region of the soul, and of the intelligence, so also for the Hero who suffers for his country, and the friend for his friend. If they know and are conscious that they are heroes, something is lacking to the divine self abnegation, and they have not entered into the plane of perfection, and the accomplishment of duty. Even in devoting themselves they regard humanity, *not as an end*, but as a means. Their sacrifice is not wholly disinterested, and therefore not conformed to the superior law of morality, which is recognised by the true philosopher in which true joy is to be found. Thus the principle of excellence reconciles itself to the community of essence which finds in it, its perfection and necessary complement.

M. Janet examines one by one all the Schools in England and Germany which oppose themselves to his views, analysing and refuting them as he progresses. He pauses especially in presence of Mr. Bain, who says, "it is useful, it is wise to act according to the approval of opinion and not to do what she blames." Yes, says M. Janet: "From that fact that there are amongst human actions some that I approve and others that I disapprove, it must be concluded that I have a certain rule according to which I approve or disapprove. There is therefore a rule superior to the things which judges of them by opinion, and superior also to the opinion which judges it. But this is only the first step of M. Janet. This rule which directs us in our appreciation of ourselves and others, what is it? Each of us possesses it in ourselves, spontaneously and instinctively we compare our own or the actions of others with an ideal we have within us of those actions, which ideal we require to be filled entirely. I have an ideal of a witness who will not lie, of a soldier who will not fly from his post, of a magistrate who will not bend before violence or corruption; and according to this ideal I judge of the real witness, soldier, magistrate, hero, and I approve or I disapprove of him.

"And if one believes," adds M. Janet that no particular man has possibly realised this ideal, we come to the conclusion that we have an ideal of a man in himself distinct from all individual men, and from or towards which, every man may go or approach.

M. Janet recognises that the qualities which compose the conception of this *man in-self*, are drawn from the exhibition we have had of these several qualities as they have been exhibited in man. We see men more truthful, more courageous, more noble than others, and it is the origin of our type of man.

"In each particular case" says M. Janet, "I conceive a man still nobler, this coming to me, I conceive another higher still and so on, I conceive that every man may be inferior to man as I idealise him. At the end of this *processus* I conceive a man whose excellence cannot be surpassed. *It is this double* necessity of having a type or a model superior to every particular man and, which nevertheless should not be an empty abstraction which has given birth to the grand Christian conception of a man-God. On the one hand God only can be perfect, on the other it is only man who can serve as a model for other men." One almost hears in these beautiful utterances of this rigid philosopher the cry of the Evangel. *Ecce Homo!!* M. Janet goes no further, it is probable he rejects the history of our Christ. He only shows the philosophic necessity of such an ideal and type for man. He goes no further. He limits himself in proving that religion is not a brilliant and poetic phenomenon belonging to the Youth of humanity as the Positivists say. He declares the last word of his researches to be—religion—"religion in self"—he says is—"Love of God." Humanity is weak, it requires and, it groans after the good and the perfect, it cries libera nos, it invokes "*the beneficent Being* who *drags it up out* of *sorrow and of sin.*" We can only say that the essence of religion is here in this philosophy, and the phase of it which responds best to these human needs will live so long as humanity remains in its present conditions. M. Janet devotes some time to a discussion of the casualistic doctrine of *Probabilism* but we have not space to refer to his arguments on this subject nor to those upon the "Immortality of the soul" nor of "the future life;" His chief works are these, "Upon the moral," the Family, the Philosophy of Happiness and "the History of Political science in its relations with morality" and upon the Problems of the 19th Century, all of which are worthy of careful study, all of which I would earnestly commend to you.

In the words of Fouillee, "we have seen a gradual and progressive conciliation during our day between the three great schools which represent the traditions of Kant in Germany, of Maine de Biran in France and of Hume in England. This accord has taken place, not by the destruction of these systems but by their superposition in one vast edifice, in which these diverse foundations sustain the bnilding instead of severally demolishing one the other. The first foundation is made of all, that materialism contained of positive trnth upon the necessary conditions, which Socrates and Plato called *mechanai*, aitiai *anagoaiai*, that is to say upon that mechanical liaison of phenomena from whence results the stability of the Universe.

The second foundation added by Socrates, Plato and Aristotle, responds to the harmonic liaison of creatures in their finality, from whence results the progress of the good, and the beautiful in the Universe. Antiquity knew only these two first regions in a philosophic consciousness, domains of Science and Art. She never assigned to morality a sphere absolutely her own, although morality was courageously practised by the Ancients. True Liberty and with it *true morality* was only divined by Plato *and the* Alexandrians. It was better understood in India in Persia, and in Judea but it was elevated only with Christianity into the rank of a new and renovating principle. This principle, obscured and mutilated by Roman Theology, re-established in France in Social order, and proposed as a Law to the World under the names of Liberty Equality and Fraternity, has not yet attained to a full conscience of itself in the order of philosophy.

In France to the sensual school entirely absorbed in the mechanism of sensations there succeeded Main de Biran who re-established in man and Nature the dynamism of Life. Victor Cousin and Descartes preserved and developed these ideas. The directing idea of the philosophy of France being that of Liberty and therefore of fraternity, is the present directing idea of Humanity itself. It has brought the tidal wave of Republicanism! In England the order of philosophy has only so far followed the material mechanism of sensations, or of phenomena; but its more recent philosophers have re-established under the external envelope of things, an internal dynamism of which the principle force is muscular energy, and this doctrine recalls the teachings of Maine de Biran :-at the same time some of the English Thinkers who are less strange to systematic views upon the whole of things, represent the universal liaison of movements as an Evolution and a Progress. This introduces into the world the idea of finality and of harmony: In the social sphere the English have a lively sense of political liberty, but moral liberty is still absent from their philosophy. It results that Liberty is for men only a means not an End: it is only valuable as it is more useful as an instrument of individual or collective well-being. Therefore the directing Idea of the English philosophy is UTILITY. For France Liberty is not a means in view of Universal Life as the Germans conceive to-day; it is not a means in view of individual Utility as the English conceive it; it is not simply a means in view of the life to come and the interests of salvation as many Christian conceive it; *it is by* itself *and in itself and for itself* a *good an End*, a *Law*; it is by itself holy and amiable; in the present life, it begins the Kingdom of God, by the realisation of Law and human solidarity; Liberty is justice, is charity, is Religion, it nnites God to man, and man to God. If freewill is an illusion, law and fraternity lose their absolute value; Law would be only a stronger force, or a minor interest; disinterestedness and Love would be only an egoistic satisfaction of an irresistible nature and of a fatal desire. Truth and Beauty in the Universe would be purchased at the expense of goodness. Antiquity seeking to explain mind by nature figured it only as a chance or Destiny, that is to say as Necessity. After thus being Chained to Nature, intelligence has delivered itself in conceiving a free morality as the only force capable of realising a Universal Love.

In Fouillee's splendid words. "Prometheus seemed forever fixed upon the hard rock of *matter:* the bonds of Necessity enveloped him on every side; He looked about him, and saw nothing which could compel his chains to fall; his first thought is a thought of discouragement, his first words are lamentations; "Immense ether, winds of rapid wings, sources of Rivers, innumerable undulations of seawaves, behold how the Gods treat a God."

It seemed as if the day would never come which was to terminate his tortures.--Nevertheless in this captive body a thought was dwelling which knew no limits, which subdued all things even the future to its own Laws, which penetrated into the secrets of necessity itself, which dominated over Time, Space and numbers, the dwelling places of servitude, and which looked into the Infinite, the sphere of Liberty. This idea of Liberty is the inextinguishable spark stolen from the fire of the Gods; To this idea responds a desire which nothing limited can satisfy; but this insatiable desire, which made the agony of Prometheus, prepared also for his deliverance; the God though enslaved bore already Liberty in his thought and in his heart. Necessity, begun to be vanquished the day when she was fully understood; knowing how the bonds were *tied,* was knowing how to untie them, one after another Prometheus unloosed them; by science, by arts, he rendered his Chains more and more flexible and regained little by little the liberty of movement. Nevertheless though attenuated and nearly invisible, he still felt them,–he felt them always,–at the same time that he saw himself thus enveloped, he beheld all other men likewise chained: He saw them strive vainly: He saw those suffering who had received the fire from heaven: He heard all around him not only the groanings of Nature but those of all Humanity, an ocean whose plaintive lamentations replied to his own sad cries: He forgot himself in listening to the voices of his brothers; in perceiving their chains he lost sight of his own fetters; his thought, and his heart fled towards them; he wished to help them. But a last and an inflexible bond restrained him still; an invulnerable obstacle separated him from those he wished to save at the cost of self-sacrifice. All at once the miracle which thought and desire attempted in vain, was accomplished by a supreme ray of LOVE. In wishing to unloose the chains from his brothers, Prometheus felt that his own had fallen. He was near to them, He was one with them; He was FREE."

We have followed carefully thus far the analysis of M. Paul Janet and others adding what seemed needful for its intelligibility for American hearers, but we may say of ourselves, acknowledging frankly all the defects and omissions of this modern Spiritualistic philosophy that it is a great gain to have fixed so much, to have restored to the world, the thoughts of God, the soul, immortality, not though supernatural Revelation, but though inflexible laws of Logic and strict philosophy as these Philosophers have done. After following with critical eyes, their close, pure and inexorable Logic, their cold, calm discussion of the Laws of thought and of Life, one realises the immense obligation under which the Philosophers of France have placed all thoughtful earnest and DOUBTING minds, by giving back to the world in clearly illuminated Text the grand words uttered by the unconscious lips of the Earth from her infancy, proclaimed alike by the sages of India, the Priests of Egypt, the Philosophers of Greece, the singers and Prophets of Israel. In a word this fundamental Truth given as the Key to all Existences.

"I God am," and there is none else and nothing else besides me."

This task is accomplished by the present philosophy of the University of France and this is the word of order in their Battalions, "all is filled with God, is full of Spirit."

We live not in the midst of Death, but of eternally metamorphosing Life! Not in a dead but a living Universe, and if in the midst of our small, busy, fretful restless existences, we would pause for a second to listen however carelessly to the seeming silence of the Infinite around about us, a silence caused not by the lack of the tones of Life; but by their infinite interceptions, interruptions, and interferences, their ceaseless rush of vital activities crossing, mingling, interchanging eternally. We would hear the deep, intense pulsations of living force which are the heart-beats of the Life of God. And the words which come echoing across the Ocean to us, from the lips of the Philosophers of the University of France, a clarion cry which our souls respond to fully.

S. A. DORSEY.

www.ingramcontent.com/pod-product-compliance
Lightning Source LLC
LaVergne TN
LVHW011132110826
845150LV00008B/2308
9781418195007